THE LONG VIEW INTO SPACE

SEYMOUR SIMON

THE LONG VIEW INTO SPACE

CROWN PUBLISHERS, INC. | NEW YORK

Published simultaneously in Canada by General Publishing Company Limited.

10 9 8 7 6 5 4 3 2

The text of this book is set in 14 point Baskerville. The illustrations are black-and-white photographs.

Library of Congress Cataloging in Publication Data

Simon, Seymour.   The long view into space.   Summary: An illustrated discussion of the planets and bodies such as moons, comets, and meteoroids found in our solar system. Also outlines the relationship the solar system has with the galaxies. 1. Solar system—Juvenile literature. [1. Solar system] I. Title.   QB46.S54   1979   523.2   79-11388
ISBN 0-517-53659-5

INTRODUCTION

Each day of our lives we travel through space on planet Earth. Space is almost empty for thousands of miles until the moon. Millions of miles away from Earth and the moon is Venus—the closest planet to Earth. And millions and millions of miles farther away is the sun.

Far more distant than the sun are the stars. And even more distant are other objects in the universe. In this book we will take a long look into deep space.

EARTH IN SPACE

Here is how our planet Earth looks from a spaceship. The light places are the tops of clouds. The dark places are land and sea. Earth belongs to a family in space called the solar system.

The sun is the center of the solar system. Nine planets circle the sun. Earth is the third planet from the sun.

The solar system is part of an even larger family. The sun is just one of a huge group of stars called the Milky Way Galaxy. Compared to the Milky Way Galaxy, the solar system is just a tiny, tiny speck.

But that's not the end. Looking through powerful telescopes we can see millions and millions of other galaxies far off in distant space. And each of the galaxies contains millions and millions of stars just as the Milky Way does.

We can learn something about stars and planets by looking at them with our eyes. But to study them in detail we must use instruments.

Telescopes are the most useful of all an astronomer's instruments. They show stars that are too faint for the eye to see. They show details of the planets and other objects in space. Astronomers take photographs of the night sky through telescopes. Most of the photographs in this book were taken through telescopes or from spaceships.

Spaceships carrying telescopes, television cameras, and other instruments travel beyond Earth's atmosphere where the viewing is very good. Some spaceships pass or even land on the moon and on the planets.

Our planet Earth, the solar system, the Milky Way, and all the other galaxies in space make up the universe. Everything in space is part of the universe.

EARTH AND ITS MOON

The land you see in the lower part of the photograph is the surface of the moon. Earth is just above the moon's surface.

The moon travels around Earth. The moon is Earth's satellite. A satellite is an object that travels around another object.

Some of the planets have several satellites, which are also called moons. But when people talk about "the moon" they usually mean Earth's moon.

The moon is Earth's nearest neighbor in space. It is about one quarter of a million miles away. That's very close for space. The planets are many million miles away, and the stars are so far away that measuring their distance in miles is not very helpful. It would be like trying to measure the distance between New York and London in inches.

The moon is so close to Earth that we can see many details on its surface. But this photograph of the moon was taken through a telescope. The brighter parts are hills and mountains covered by large holes called craters. The dark parts are flat lands that are called seas. Early peoples thought that these dark spaces were covered with water. Today we know that they are really dry lands, but we still call them seas.

Until a short time ago no one had ever seen the other side of the moon. That's because the same side of the moon always faces Earth. Then, a few years ago, spaceships from Earth passed behind the moon. Here is a photograph that shows part of the far side of the moon. It has craters and mountains, much like the side we see from Earth. But it has few flat lands, or seas.

As the moon circles Earth it reflects the light of the sun and we see different portions of it. It looks as if the moon is changing shape. We call these different shapes the moon's phases. This photograph shows a phase called a crescent moon.

The photograph below shows the surface of the moon. The round circle at the bottom left of the photograph is a crater. It is called Copernicus after the famous astronomer. Astronomers think the crater was formed when a huge rock crashed into the surface of the moon many years ago. Many other craters can also be seen in this photograph.

The smooth areas covering most of the photograph are seas. They look as smooth as water because they are covered by a layer of dust. Seas are the largest features on the moon; we can easily see them without a telescope.

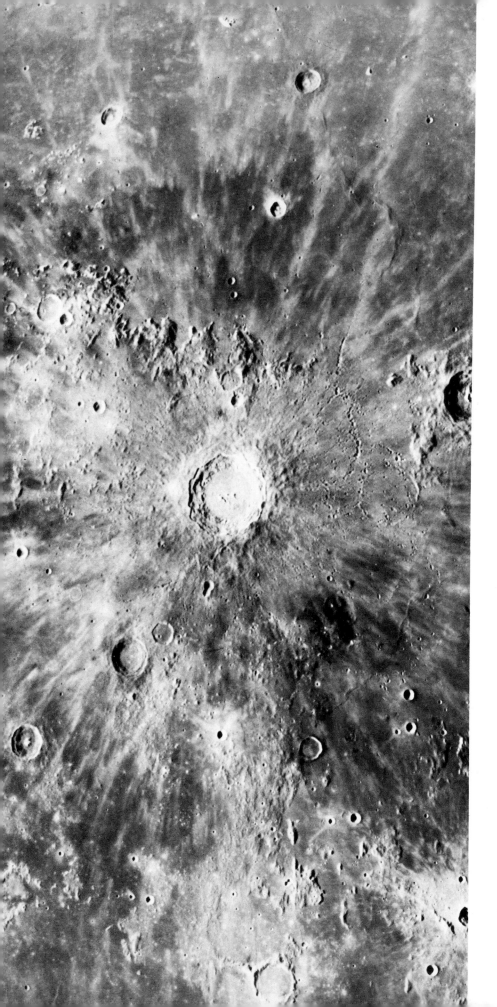

Here is an even closer look at the surface of the moon and the crater Copernicus. Copernicus is at the center of the photograph. The walls of the crater slope steeply to the floor, which is thousands of feet below. At the center of the crater floor are several mountain peaks.

The bright streaks around Copernicus are called rays. The rays stretch out across the surface of the moon for hundreds of miles. Scientists think that they were formed by the large rock that formed Copernicus. The rock crashed into the moon and scattered lunar dust and rock in all directions.

In this photograph we can see hundreds of smaller craters around Copernicus. Even the tiny black dots are craters. Over 30,000 craters have been counted on the side of the moon that we can see from Earth.

This photograph of Copernicus was taken from a spaceship that was twenty-eight miles above it. The black lines were caused by the television camera that sent the photograph to Earth. The dark shape at the bottom of the photo is a small crater that is outside Copernicus. The mountains at the top of the photo are the walls of Copernicus. The distance from the small crater to the mountains is about thirty miles.

The astronauts who first visited the moon landed a few hundred miles away from Copernicus. They found a strange, dead place. One of them took this photograph. We can see the dust and rocks that make up the moon's surface. On the moon there are no winds, no clouds, no rain, no weather. But the moon has terrible temperatures. It is either burning hot or freezing cold.

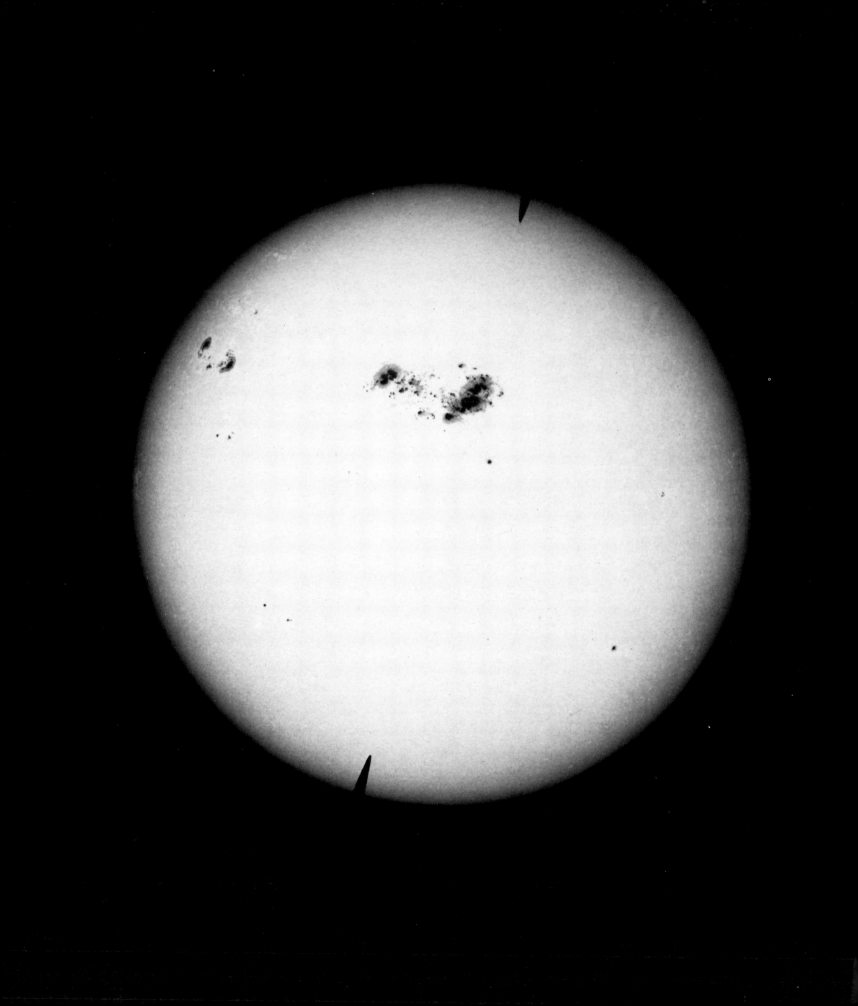

THE SUN AND THE SOLAR SYSTEM

The sun is far away from Earth and its moon. A spaceship that could travel to the moon in a few days would take more than a year to come close to the sun.

The sun is an average-size star. There is nothing very special about it, except for the fact that it is our star. Life on Earth depends upon the heat and light of the sun.

If we were to compare the size of the sun in this photograph to that of Earth, Earth would be as big as the period that follows this sentence. The black marks on the surface of the sun are raging storms called sunspots. Earth could easily be swallowed up in one sunspot.

The sun is at the center of our solar system. Nine planets travel around the sun. The closest planets to the sun are Mercury, Venus, Earth, and Mars. They are sometimes called the Inner Planets. The Outer Planets are Jupiter, Saturn, Uranus, Neptune, and Pluto.

If you wanted to make a scale model of the sun and the most distant solar planet, a basketball would be the sun, and Pluto would be a grain of sand placed nearly a mile away.

The sun is made up of hot gases, and its surface is never still. The gases toss and spin constantly. At times, the gases shoot up from the surface. They are called prominences. The prominence in this photograph of the sun is over 200,000 miles high. A prominence may last for hours, or days, or weeks. Then it becomes smaller and smaller until it finally disappears.

This photograph was taken during a time when the moon blocked out the sun. We call this a solar eclipse. The halo of light around the sun is called the corona. The word corona means "crown." The corona is the outer part of the sun's gases. It is brightest close to the sun, and it fades as it gets farther away. Parts of the corona can reach millions of miles into space.

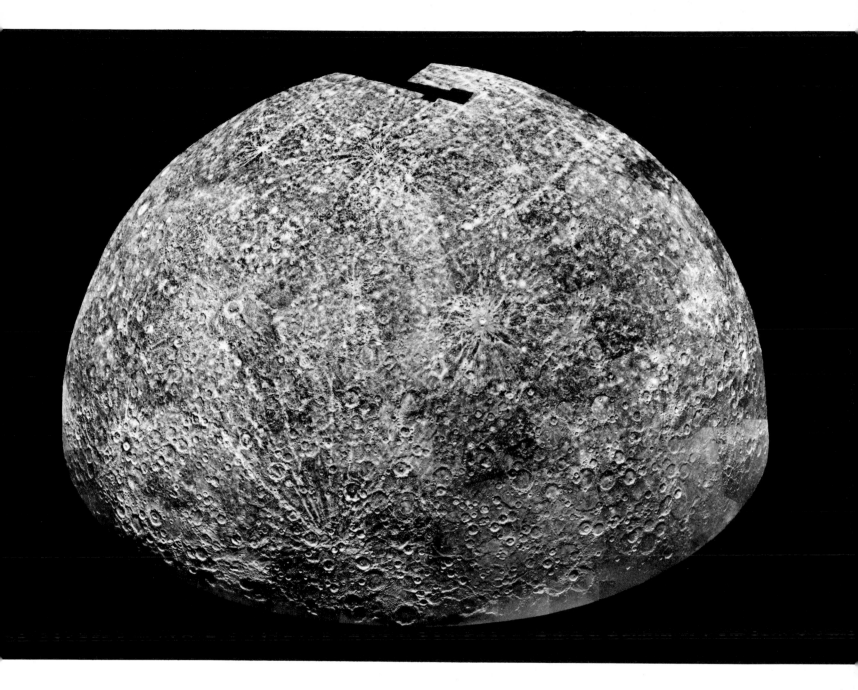

Mercury is the closest planet to the sun. It is also the smallest planet, less than half the width of Earth. A long time ago, Mercury had a blanket of gases around it. But Mercury is so small and so hot that the gases boiled away long ago. On the surface of Mercury there are craters, mountains, and flat lands. The surface is much like that of our own moon. This is a photograph of a model of Mercury. Many photographs of Mercury were taken from a spaceship. The photographs were then combined to make this model.

Venus is the second planet from the sun; Earth is the third. Venus is about the same size as Earth. It comes closer to Earth than any other planet. It is covered by thick clouds of gas, which trap the heat of the sun. The trapped heat makes the surface of Venus hot enough to melt certain metals. This photograph was taken by a camera in a spaceship passing close to Venus.

Venus changes its shape just like the moon. This photograph shows Venus in a crescent phase.

Venus shines very brightly. Some nights it is the first object to appear in the sky. Other nights it is the last object to disappear in the morning. Early peoples called Venus the evening star or the morning star. But Venus is not a star—it is a planet.

Mars is the fourth planet from the sun. It is a small planet, a little over half the width of Earth. Because of its reddish color in the night sky, Mars is sometimes called the Red Planet.

This photograph of the surface of Mars was taken through a telescope. You can see fuzzy patches of dark and light. These patches change in color and size as Mars goes from summer to winter, but we are not sure of the reasons for these changes.

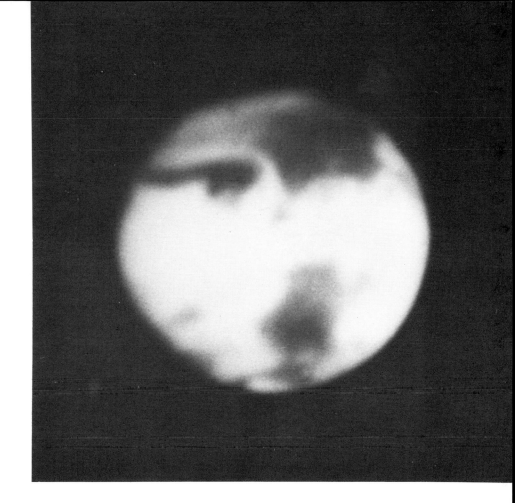

This is a photograph of a model of Mars. We can see that the surface of Mars is covered with craters and mountains.

Spaceships have landed on Mars. They have found that Mars has a very thin layer of air. Some people thought that the spaceships would find life on Mars. But no traces of life have been found so far.

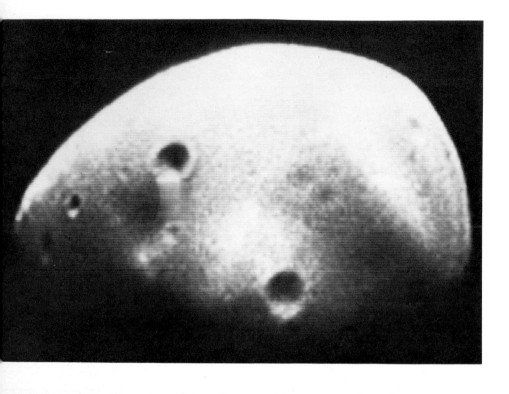

Mars has two moons, called Phobos and Deimos. Both of them are small lumps of rock marked with craters. This photograph of Deimos was made by combining two photographs that were taken from a spaceship.

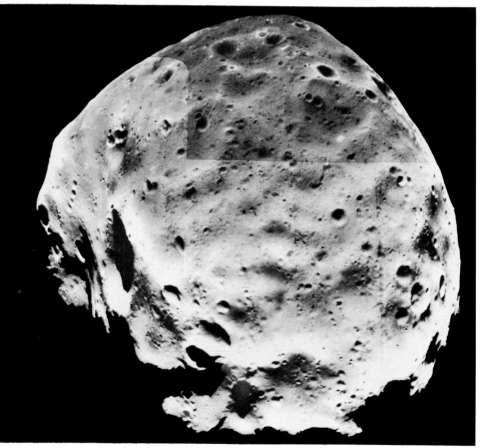

A number of smaller photographs were combined to make this picture of Phobos. Phobos travels very quickly around Mars. Someone living on Mars would see Phobos rise and set three times a day. No other moon in the solar system travels so quickly.

Jupiter is the fifth planet from the sun. It is made up of gases. It is also the largest planet in the solar system. If Jupiter were the size of a basketball, then Earth would be the size of a marble. Jupiter has thirteen moons—more than any other planet. It has a ring around it that is made up of large boulders and other space debris.

This photograph of Jupiter was taken through a telescope. The light and dark areas are called bands. The bands are the tops of clouds. Jupiter spins so quickly that its clouds form bands.

One of the strangest features of Jupiter is the Great Red Spot, which we can see in the lower right of the photograph. It looks like a large eye. Earth could easily fit in it. Astronomers think it is a storm of whirling gases that has lasted for hundreds of years.

Saturn is the sixth planet from the sun. It is the second largest planet. Like Jupiter, Saturn is made up mostly of gases. Saturn is large, yet it is very light.

Saturn has beautiful flat rings around its middle. In this photograph, we can see two of the brightest rings.

The rings are made up of many, many particles of dust and ice. The particles are so close together that the rings look solid. And they are so thin that they almost disappear when we look at them from the edge. No one is sure why Saturn has rings. Scientists think the rings may have come from substances that were left over when Saturn was first formed.

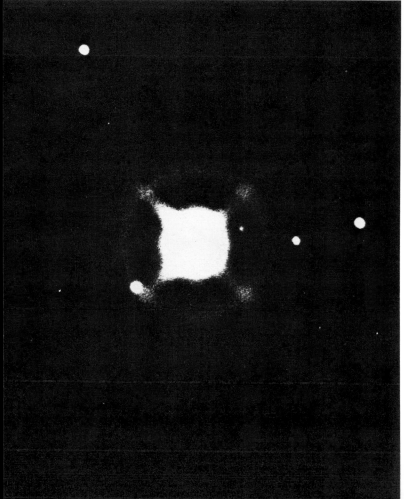

Uranus is the seventh planet from the sun. It is much bigger than Earth, but it is so far from Earth that we can barely see it without a telescope. The odd shape in the center of this photograph was caused by the telescope.

Uranus has five moons. The four largest moons look like small white circles in the photograph. The fifth moon looks like a tiny dot just to the right of Uranus. None of the moons is as large as Earth's moon.

Like Jupiter and Saturn, Uranus is made up of gases. And like Saturn, Uranus has rings around it, but they are too faint to be seen in this photograph.

Neptune, the eighth planet from the sun, is almost a twin of Uranus. It is just a bit larger than Uranus, and it is made up of the same kind of gases. But Neptune is much farther out in space than Uranus.

This photograph of Neptune was taken through a large telescope. The spikes of light around Neptune were caused by the telescope. Neptune has two moons. The arrow in the upper-right-hand corner of the photograph points to one of them.

Most of the time Pluto is the farthest planet from the sun, but from 1979 to 1999 it will be a little closer to the sun than Neptune. Pluto is so far away that these photographs, which were taken through one of the largest telescopes on Earth, show Pluto as only a point of light. The arrows in each photograph point to Pluto. If you compare Pluto's position in the two photographs, you can see that it moved.

Pluto is a small planet made up of rock and frozen gas. Some astronomers think that it was once a moon of Neptune. They think that the moon broke away from Neptune and began to circle the sun on its own. When that happened, Pluto became the ninth planet in the solar system.

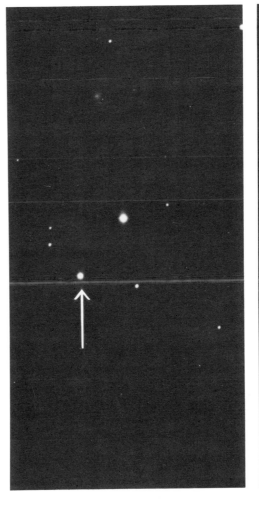
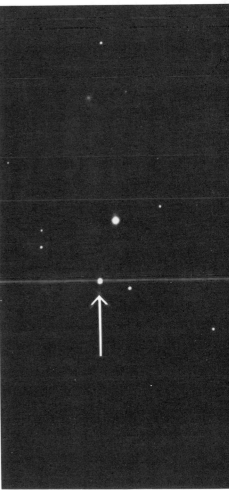

Along with planets and their moons, comets and meteoroids also circle the sun.

Comets are made up of frozen gases and dust. One astronomer called comets dirty snowballs. As a comet nears the sun, the sun's rays make the gases glow and push them out to form a tail. A bright comet with a long tail is one of the most beautiful sights in the sky. The brightest comets can be seen even during the day.

One of the brightest comets is Halley's comet. The last time it approached the sun was in 1910. This photograph was taken at that time. Halley's comet should be back again in 1985 or 1986.

Comets travel around the sun in huge cigar-shaped paths. Some comets travel so far from the sun that they do not come near the sun and Earth for thousands of years.

In 1973 a bright comet called Kohoutek came close to the sun and Earth. It could be seen from Earth without a telescope for several weeks. Kohoutek is now traveling away from Earth. It won't be near Earth again for thousands of years.

Meteoroids are chunks of rock or metal that travel in odd-shaped paths around the sun. Usually we cannot see them because they are too small. But when they enter the air around Earth they become red-hot and begin to burn. Then they become bright flashes, which are called meteors. Some people call meteors shooting or falling stars. But they are not stars. The streak in the top of this photograph is the trail of a meteor that is burning up in the air.

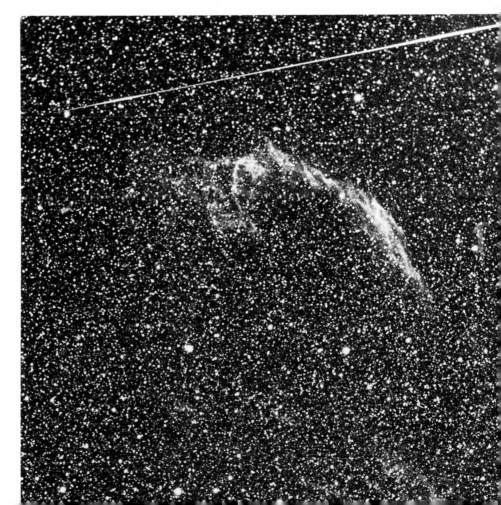

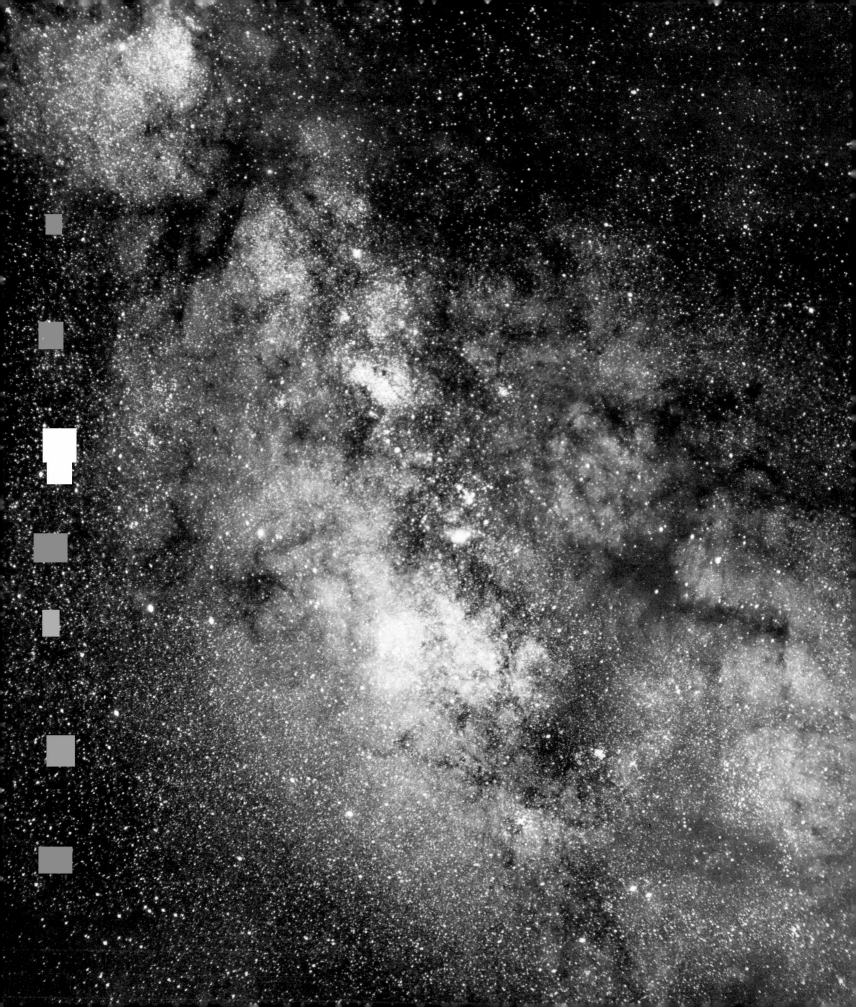

BEYOND THE
SOLAR SYSTEM

The stars you see in the night sky are far beyond the solar system. Some of them are so far away from Earth that the light from them blends together. They look like clouds of pale white light stretching across the sky. These stars belong to the Milky Way.

The Milky Way is part of a very large group of stars called a galaxy. Our sun is one of these stars. The sun, its planets, moons, comets, and meteoroids are only a tiny part of our galaxy, which is called the Milky Way Galaxy.

This photograph shows one small part of the Milky Way. You can see that it is really millions of stars. The stars look small and close together, but each star is far away from its nearest neighbor. They look small and close together because they are far from Earth.

There are over 100 billion stars in the Milky Way. If someone wanted to count the stars and counted one each second, it would take more than three thousand years to count them all.

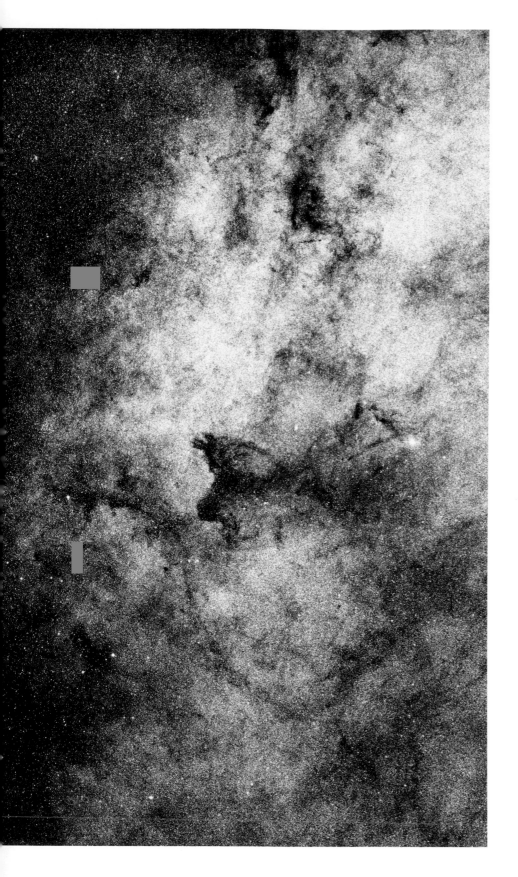

The stars we see in the night sky look like twinkling points of light. That is because they are so far away from us. Stars are great globes of hot, bright gases. Only the sun is close enough for us to see what stars are really like.

The sun is an ordinary star. There are many stars that are about the same size and color. But there are many, many stars that are different from the sun. Some are giant red stars, much larger than the sun. Others are white dwarf stars even smaller than Earth. Some stars are very hot and some stars are cool. Some stars are blue and some stars are gold. There are many different kinds of stars in our galaxy.

Earth turns like a giant spinning top. Watching the stars is like watching one's surroundings from a seat on a merry-go-round. The photograph at the right is of the night sky. It was taken over several hours. As Earth turned, the camera turned with it. The stars made circular trails on the film.

This photo of the constellation Orion, the Hunter, was taken through a small telescope. The row of three bright stars forms Orion's belt. Orion can be seen in the winter sky.

Constellations are groups of stars that appear to form patterns in the night sky. People of long ago named the constellations after gods, heroes, and other figures in their myths.

Seen from Earth, the stars in the constellations look as though they are close together. But each star in a constellation may be very far from its neighbor.

Below is a photograph of the Big Dipper. The Big Dipper is part of a constellation called Ursa Major, or the Big Bear. The next to the last star in the handle of the Big Dipper is a double star. Two stars close together are called double stars, or binaries. Binary stars circle around each other.

The brighter of the two stars in this photograph is Mizar. The fainter star is Alcor. A long time ago, the stars were used to test the eyesight of soldiers. Those soldiers who could see Alcor became scouts.

Some stars are close to each other in space. These groups of stars are called star clusters. This photograph shows a bright star cluster. It is named the Pleiades, or the Seven Sisters.

On a clear, moonless night, it is possible to see seven of the stars in the Pleiades. But with a telescope we can see more than one hundred. Taken through a telescope, this photograph shows some of the brightest stars in the Pleiades. The stars are surrounded by a glowing haze of dust and gases. We call this haze nebulosity.

Some star clusters contain thousands and thousands of stars that are very close together. Astronomers call these globular clusters. The two large white spots in this photograph show a double globular cluster. They contain millions of stars. The stars are so close together that we cannot see each individual star.

Imagine yourself on a planet circling a star in the middle of a globular cluster. The sky would look different from the way it does on Earth. A brilliant blaze of stars would light up the sky and turn night into day.

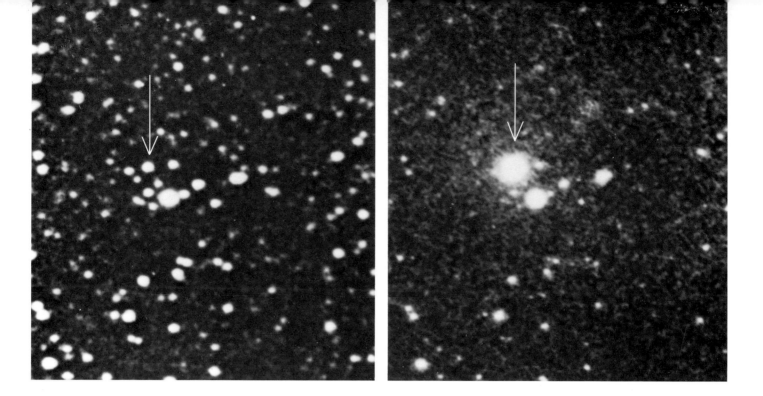

Sometimes a star flares up in the night sky. It becomes thousands of times brighter within a few hours or a few days. From Earth it looks as if a bright new star has appeared. Early astronomers called these stars novae, from a Latin word that means "new." We know now that a nova is really a dim star that has suddenly exploded.

The white arrow in the photograph at the left points to a dim star. The white arrow in the photograph at the right points to the same star a few weeks later when it became a nova. After it flared up, the star returned to its normal brightness.

Supernovae are stars that explode and rip themselves apart. They become millions of times brighter. Supernovae are very rare. The last supernova seen from Earth flared up over three hundred years ago.

In between the stars, there are small amounts of dust and gases. In some places, the dust and gases are thicker, and they form a cloud. We call these clouds nebulae, from a Latin word that means "mist" or "cloud."

The photograph at the right is of the Great Nebula in the constellation Orion. The mass of gas and dust that you see stretches a great distance across space. Nebulae do not shine by themselves. They are lit by stars that are nearby or within them. The Great Nebula in Orion has a number of hot stars that shine within it.

Some nebulae glow brightly. Here are three photographs of bright nebulae. The photograph at the left shows the Diffuse Nebula in the constellation of Dorado. The photograph below shows a nebula in the constellation of Monoceros.

This is a photograph of the Lagoon Nebula, which is in the constellation of Sagittarius.

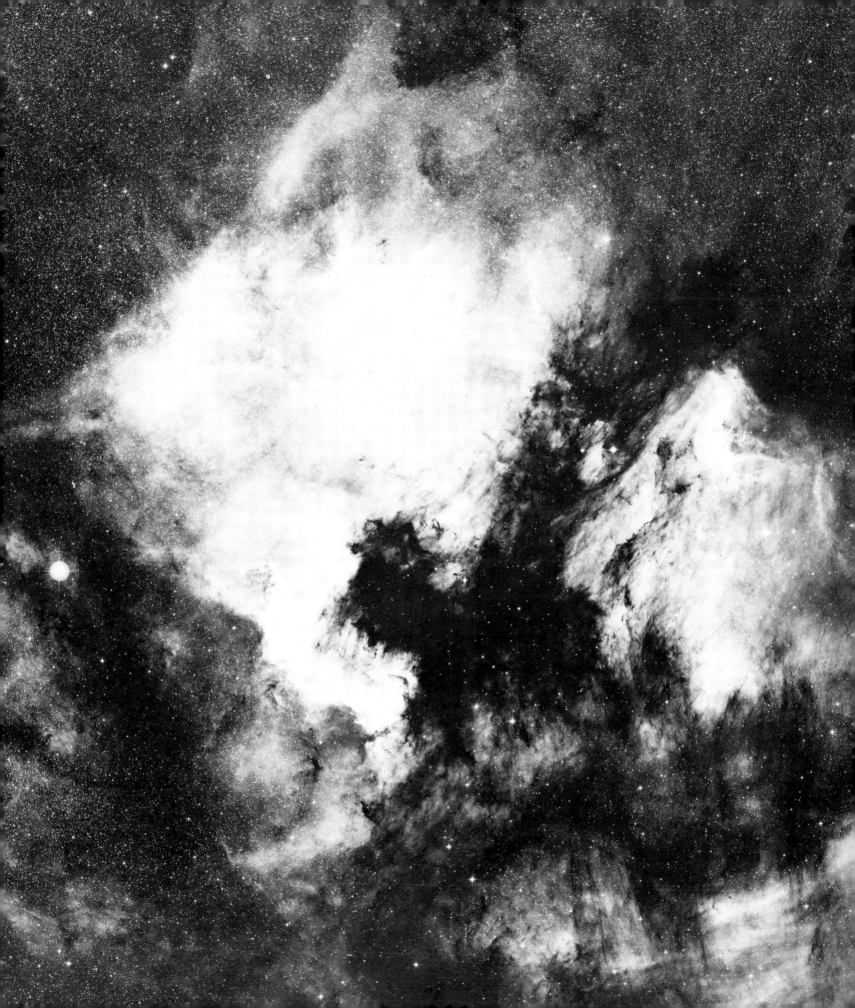

Some nebulae are dark. There are no stars nearby to make them glow. They are called dark nebulae or coal sacks. We can see the outlines of dark nebulae because they block out the light of the stars behind them. The photograph at the left is of the North American Nebula in the constellation of Cygnus.

The photograph at the right is of the Horsehead Nebula in the constellation of Orion.

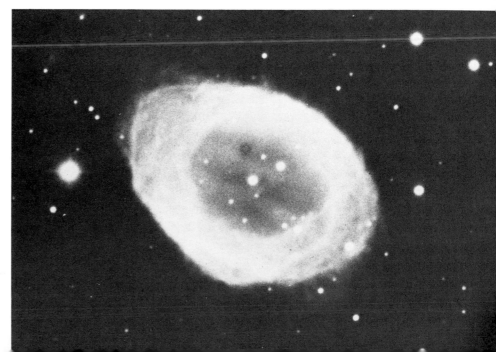

This is a photograph of the Ring Nebula in the constellation of Lyra. It looks like a smoke ring around a star.

BEYOND THE MILKY WAY GALAXY

This is a photograph of a galaxy that is billions of miles away from Earth and the Milky Way Galaxy. It is called the Great Galaxy, and it is in the constellation of Andromeda. There are millions of galaxies that are even farther away from the Milky Way. Each of these galaxies contains billions of stars.

There are also millions of smaller galaxies in space that are called dwarf galaxies. Each dwarf galaxy contains thousands of stars.

With a powerful telescope we can see what the Great Galaxy in Andromeda looks like. We can see that it is an "island" of stars, star clusters, and nebulae, just like our own galaxy.

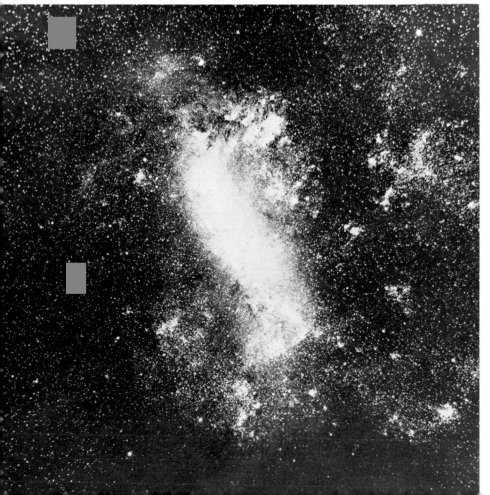

The Large Magellanic Cloud is a galaxy that is the Milky Way's nearest neighbor. It looks like a bright cloud in the night sky. It is irregular in shape and much smaller than our own galaxy. There are millions and millions of stars in the Large Magellanic Cloud.

Through telescopes we can see that galaxies have several different shapes.
Some galaxies have no special shape, and they are called irregular galaxies.
This is a photograph of an irregular galaxy.

These three photographs show spiral galaxies. They look like giant pinwheels. The Milky Way Galaxy is a spiral galaxy. The stars are grouped together in arms that spiral outward from the center.

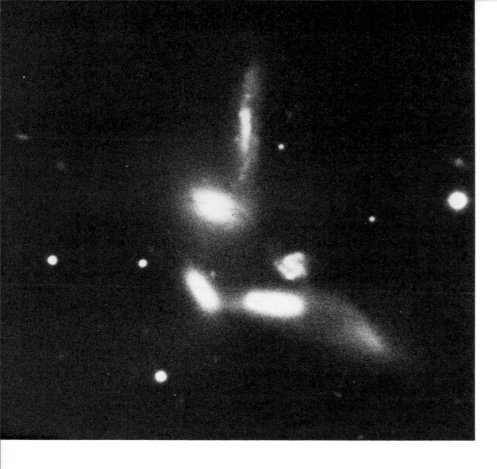

This is a photograph of elliptical galaxies. They look like flattened balls.

Through powerful telescopes we can see galaxies in every direction in space.

Here is a group of galaxies that are so far away that they can barely be photographed through even the largest telescopes.

All of the galaxies make up the universe. Everybody and everything is part of the universe. If you wanted to write your return address on a letter to be carried by a spaceship, it might look something like this:

Name:
Street:
Town or City:
State:
Country:
Planet: *Earth*
System: *Solar*
Galaxy: *Milky Way*

You are truly a citizen of the universe.

PICTURE CREDITS

The author wishes to acknowledge for the use of photographs:

Hale Observatories: 10 (top), 11 (top and bottom), 12, 14, 16 (top and bottom), 18 (bottom), 19 (top), 21, 22 (top), 23 (bottom), 24, 25 (top), 26, 28, 30 (top), 33, 34 (bottom), 36, 37 (top and bottom), 38, 40 (top), 41, 43 (top), 44 (top and bottom), 46

Kitt Peak National Observatory: frontispiece, 31 (top and bottom), 34 (top), 35, 42, 45

NASA: 6, 8, 10 (bottom), 13 (top and bottom), 17, 18 (top), 19 (bottom), 20 (top and bottom)

Yerkes Observatory Photograph, University of Chicago: 22 (bottom), 23 (top), 25 (bottom), 29, 30 (bottom), 32, 40 (bottom), 43 (bottom)